HAL•LEONARD
Beginning PIANO SOLO PLAY-ALONG

VOL. 3

RODGERS AND HAMMERSTEIN™

THE SOUND OF MUSIC®

CONTENTS

ISBN 978-1-4584-0826-6

WILLIAMSON MUSIC®
A RODGERS AND HAMMERSTEIN COMPANY
www.williamsonmusic.com

EXCLUSIVELY DISTRIBUTED BY

HAL•LEONARD®
7777 W. BLUEMOUND RD. P.O. BOX 13819 MILWAUKEE, WI 53213

Visit Hal Leonard Online at
www.halleonard.com

DO-RE-MI

Lyrics by OSCAR HAMMERSTEIN II
Music by RICHARD RODGERS

With spirit

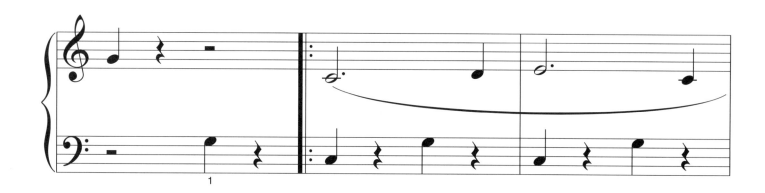

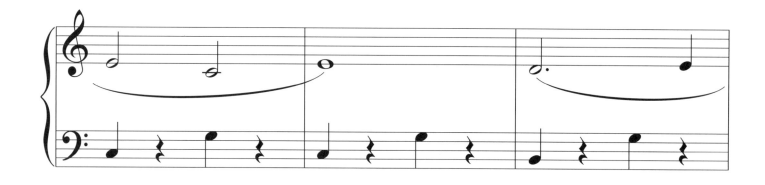

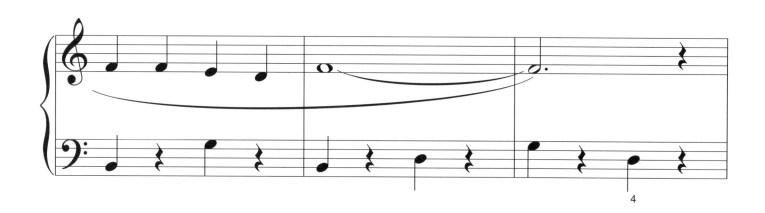

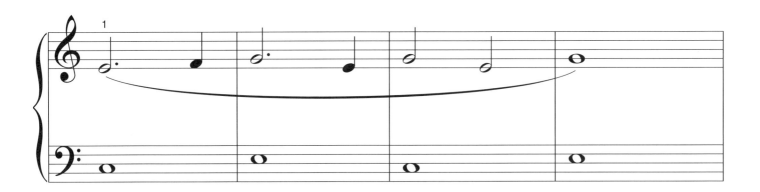

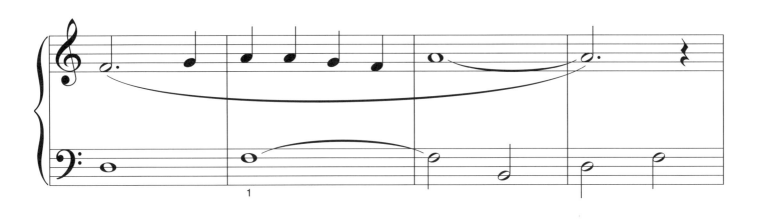

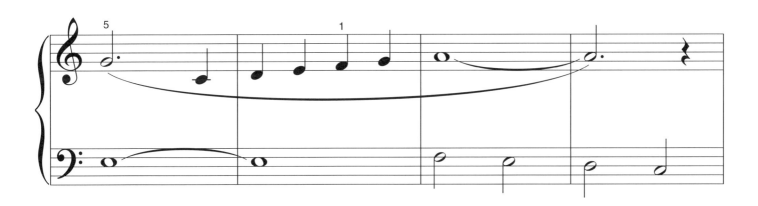

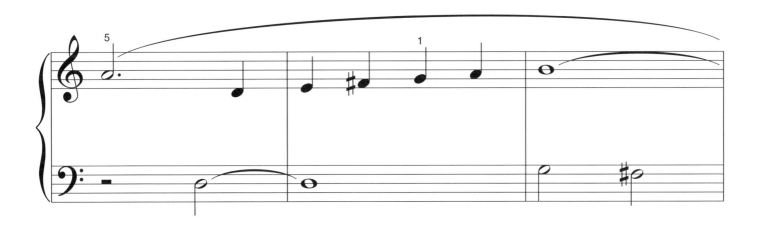

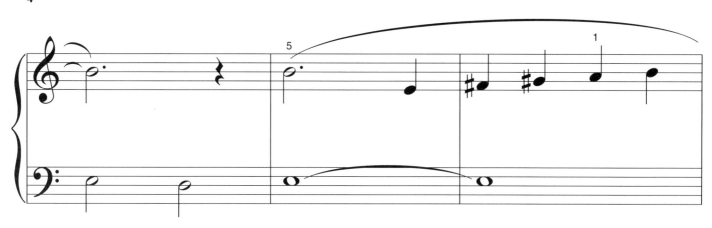

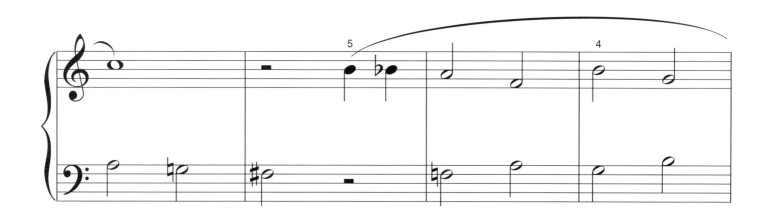

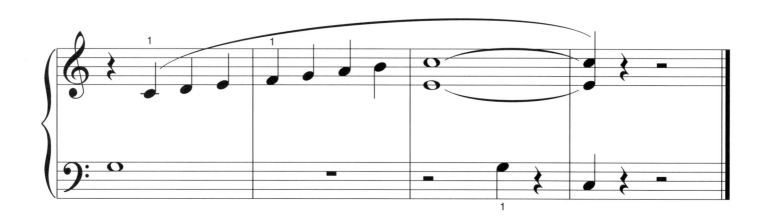

CLIMB EV'RY MOUNTAIN

Lyrics by OSCAR HAMMERSTEIN II
Music by RICHARD RODGERS

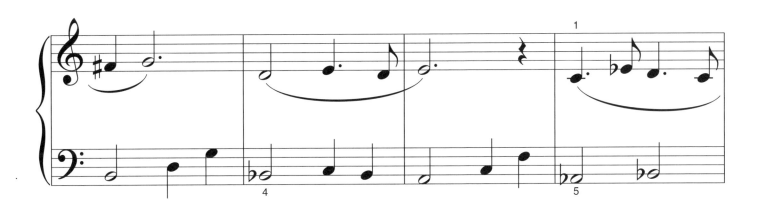

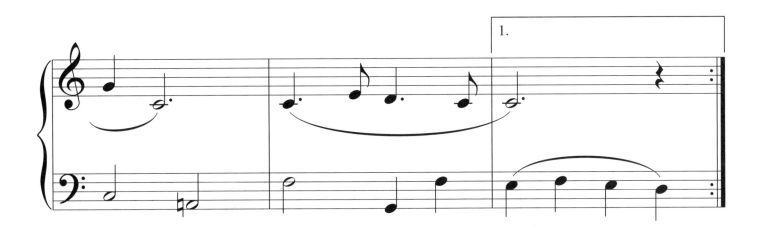

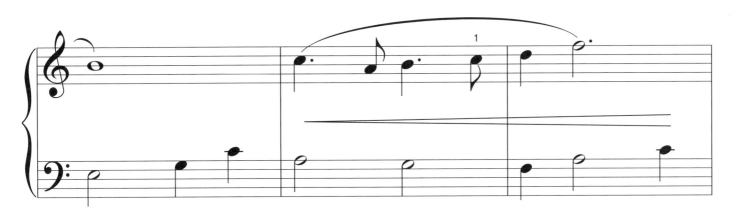

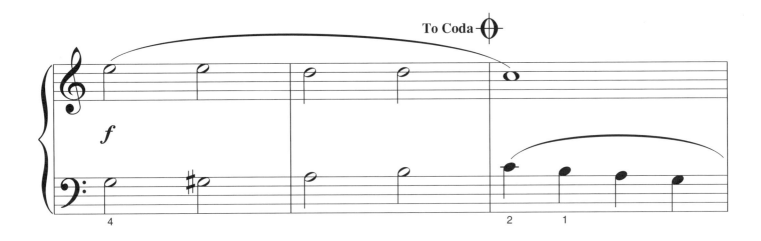

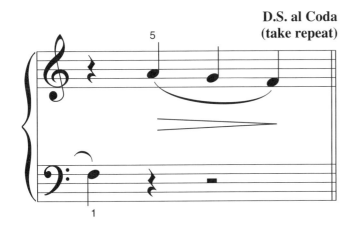

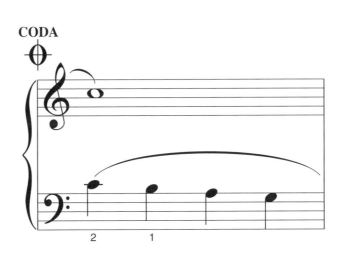

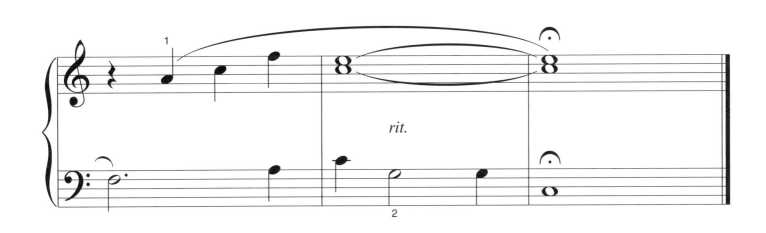

EDELWEISS

Lyrics by OSCAR HAMMERSTEIN II
Music by RICHARD RODGERS

Moderately

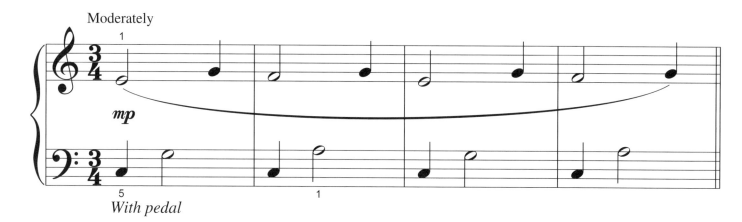

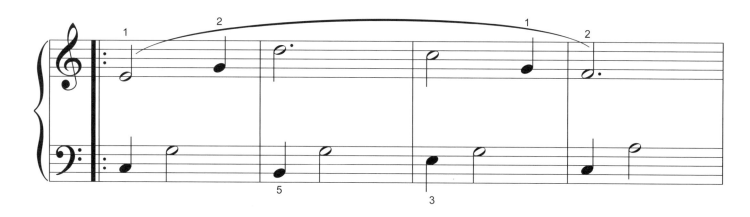

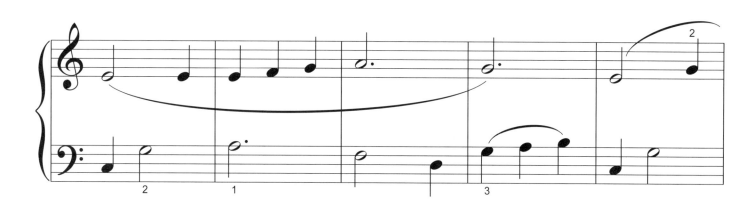

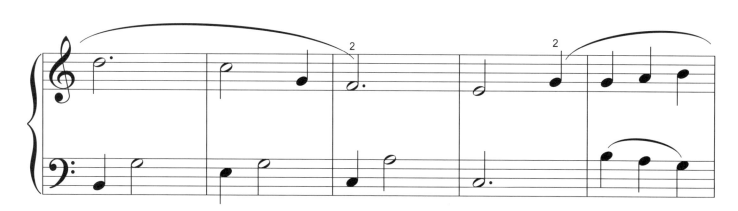

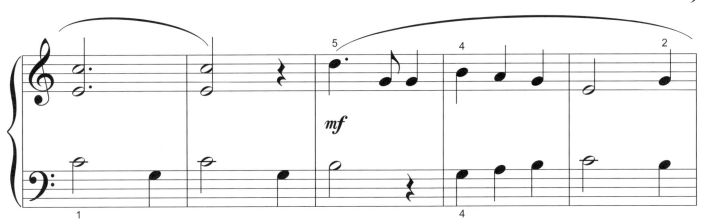

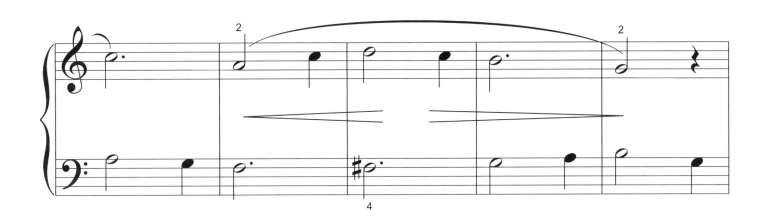

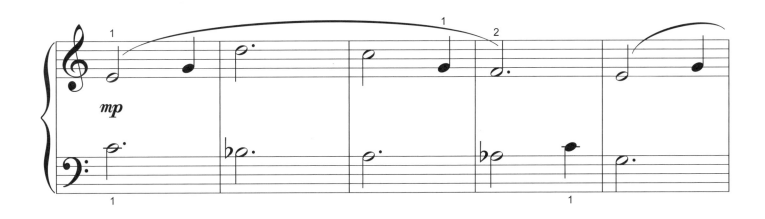

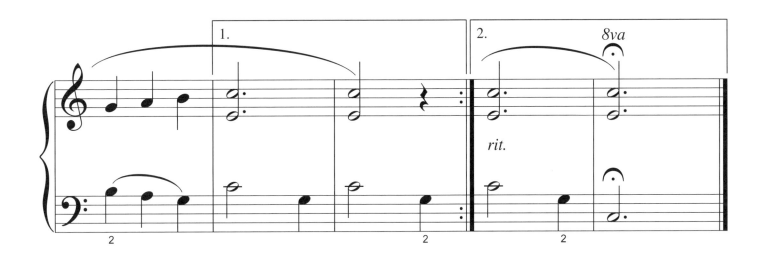

THE LONELY GOATHERD

Lyrics by OSCAR HAMMERSTEIN II
Music by RICHARD RODGERS

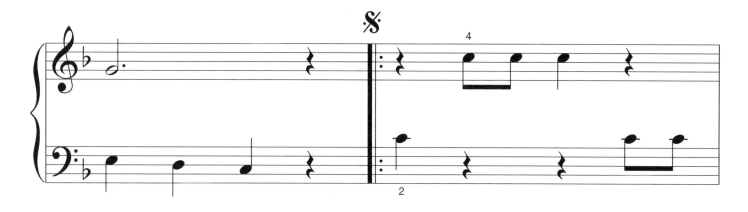

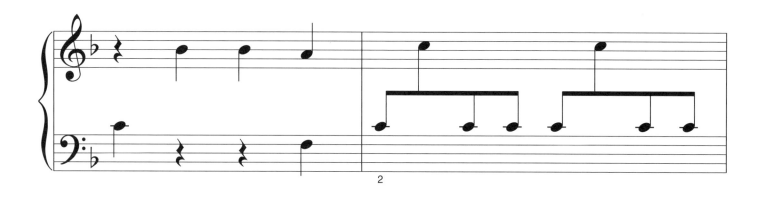

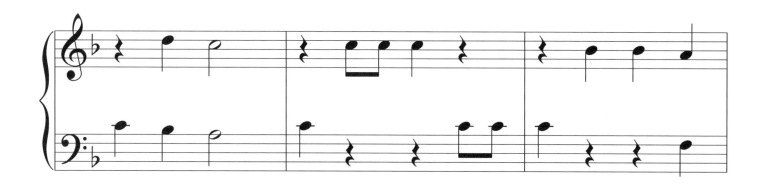

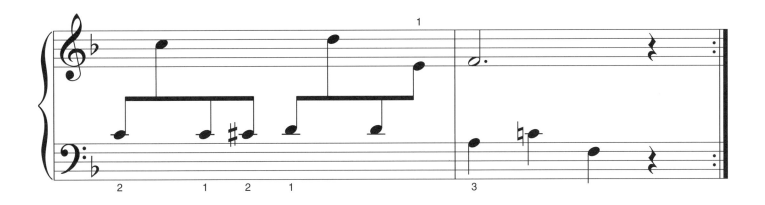

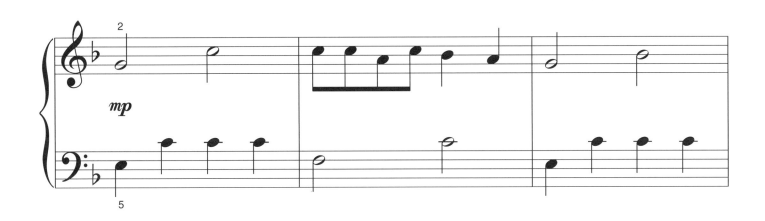

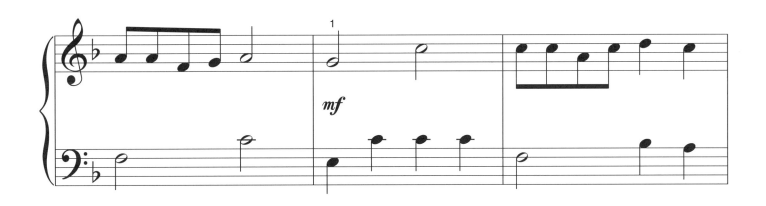

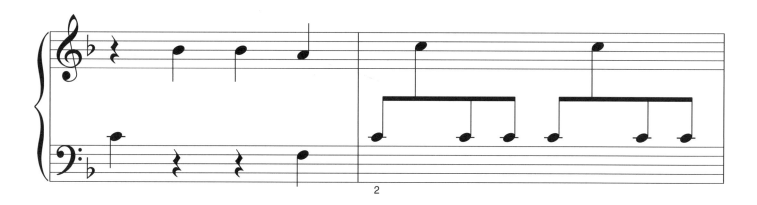

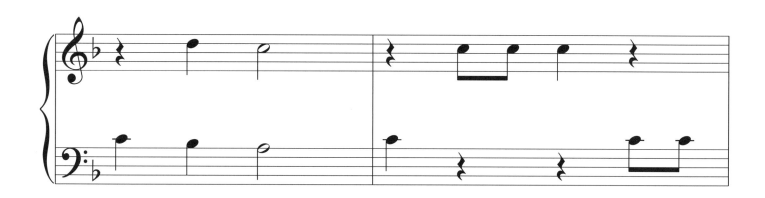

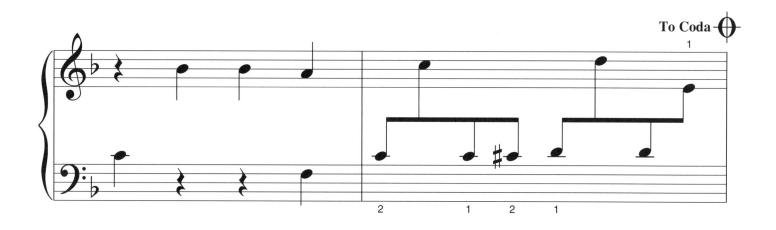

To Coda

CODA

D.S. al Coda
(no repeat)

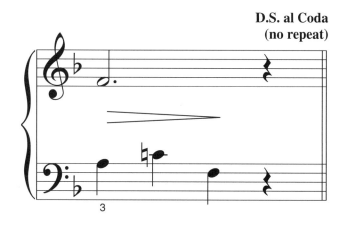

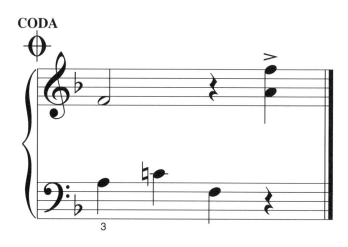

SIXTEEN GOING ON SEVENTEEN

Lyrics by OSCAR HAMMERSTEIN II
Music by RICHARD RODGERS

MARIA

Lyrics by OSCAR HAMMERSTEIN II
Music by RICHARD RODGERS

Moderately

MY FAVORITE THINGS

Lyrics by OSCAR HAMMERSTEIN II
Music by RICHARD RODGERS

SO LONG, FAREWELL

Lyrics by OSCAR HAMMERSTEIN II
Music by RICHARD RODGERS

Moderately